Mrs Marigold's Menagerie

By Jack Gabolinscy

Illustrated by Helen Bacon

Mrs Marigold's Menagerie

Frost Road, where Mrs Marigold lived, was like a centipede with a bad leg. All the houses except hers were the same – the roofs and walls were freshly painted in pale colours, the hedges neatly trimmed, the lawns mown and the shrubs and trees pruned to attractive shapes and sizes.

But not Number 27 – Mrs Marigold's home! Number 27 was the centipede's bad leg. Number 27 had a roof of striped orange and red, walls of sunbeam yellow, and windows and doors of purple. The hedges stalked about the garden with uncontrolled straggly haircuts. The lawns were waist high and the unpruned shrubs and trees, and tangled climbing roses and jasmine, made her place look like a wild Amazon jungle.

"Number 27 is an ugly blot on the neighbourhood," grumbled the man in Number 29.

"Shocking!" humphed the woman in Number 30 across the road.

"I'm writing to the mayor," growled the woman in Number 31.

"You do that," agreed her husband, flapping his arms at the peacocks in his garage.

Question:

What do you think might be in the letter to the mayor?

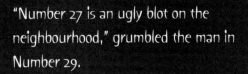

5

Mrs Marigold loved her garden. "It's taken a lifetime," she said, clumping along an overgrown path in gumboots.

And she had a large and happy "family" to fill the garden.

There was Mop, her old terrier who was deaf. There was Slink the cat. There was Captain Rainbow, the parrot, who screeched "Ooh yuk! Ooh yuk! Ooh yuk!" no matter what he was fed, and "Shut up! Shut up! Shut up!" whenever he was annoyed.

"Ooh yuk! ooh yuk! Shut up! Shut up!"

There were the fish by the porch in a fish pond, bright with lily flowers. And nobody knew how many rabbits and patchwork guinea pigs lived in the long grass.

Lastly there were the peacocks, Mrs Marigold's pride and joy. "My Royal Family," she called them.

Question:

Why do you think Mrs Marigold called the peacocks "My Royal Family"?

Night and morning Mrs Marigold fed her family. Putting her fingers to her mouth, she sent a piercing whistle echoing into every nook and cranny of the neighbourhood.

Every garden in the neighbourhood moved. Rabbits and guinea pigs scampered home. They came from 29's lettuce patch, from 41's flower seedlings; they popped out of a hole in 25's new glasshouse, and waded from the bird bath on 23's front lawn. The Royal Family flew home screeching from wherever they had been roosting.

Even the sparrows and blackbirds swooped in for a meal.

... every nook

Synonym:

A synonym is a word that means the same or nearly the same as another word.

Which word is the synonym for swooped?

A dived

B descended

C flew

A, B or C?

and every cranny

But one evening, after Mrs Marigold had fed her menagerie, the telephone rang. "Mrs Marigold, I've had enough! If you don't put your guinea pigs in a cage, I'm going to complain to the mayor. Last week they ate my spinach. Tonight they've been into my sweet peas. What will be next? Put them in cages or I will complain!"

"Shut up! Shut up! Shut up!" screeched Captain Rainbow.

"Shut up! Shut up! Shut up!"

Mrs Marigold hung the telephone up because the woman wasn't being polite. Soon it rang again. It was another angry neighbour.

Predict:

What do you think might happen in the story?

"Mrs Marigold. This is Fred Oglebump from 39. Your rabbits have just eaten my prize flowers. What are you going to do about it?"

"How do you know they were my rabbits?" asked Mrs Marigold.

"Who else has rabbits?" shouted the man into the phone.

But Mrs Marigold had hung up again. "Have another biscuit, Captain Rainbow. If you've got nothing nice to say, don't say anything at all. That's what I say."

As you can see, Mrs Marigold wasn't the most popular person in Frost Road. That is, unless you count the children.

Children loved her. They were always visiting with their teachers. They helped clean out the fish pond. They hunted through the long grass for peacock feathers, and they asked a hundred and one questions.

"Can I borrow a guinea pig for the school fair?"

"How do you teach a parrot to talk?"

"How many feathers in a peacock's tail?"

Inference:

"Children loved her."

What inferences can you make from this text about Mrs Marigold's character?

One morning, while Mrs Marigold was feeding her family, a very angry man stormed onto her porch. He waved his arms and shouted. "Those birds! They have messed on my car!"

"Calm yourself, Mr Symes. You will give yourself a heart attack. Can I make you a cup of tea?" asked Mrs Marigold.

"No! I don't want a cup of tea! I want those grubby birds!" shouted the man, and he stepped towards the peacocks.

"ScreeEEeech!! ScreeEEEeech!! Shut up! Shut up!" squawked Captain Rainbow, flying at the man's face.

"ScrEEEEEeech!!"
"ScrEEEEEeech!!"

. . . I want those grubby birds!

Back stepped the man off the porch - a perfect backward dive - into the fish pond. He stood up dripping water and leaves from his hair and clothes.

"Ooh yuk! Ooh yuk! Ooh yuk!" cackled Captain Rainbow.

The man fled from the fish pond towards the gate. "You've left your hat, Mr Symes," called Mrs Marigold, but he didn't come back.

Action and Consequence:

The man stepped back off the porch.	The man fell into the fish pond.

Find another action and consequence.

A few days later, Mrs Marigold received a letter from the mayor.
It said:

Dear Mrs Marigold,
Your neighbours have complained about your untidy garden and your wild animals.

One man has had his prize flowers eaten by your rabbits and guinea pigs. Others say your garden is an eyesore. Another man tells me he was attacked by a screaming bird and chased into a pond. He says your peacocks are always messing on his car.

As mayor, it is my job to look after our town's good name and to make sure every citizen is safe. I would like to visit you on Tuesday afternoon to investigate these serious complaints.

The Mayor
Mr Archibald Snooks.

"How nice," said Mrs Marigold to herself. "A visit from the mayor. We must see that he has a good time."

Problem and Solution:

Mrs Marigold's neighbours have complaints.	?

How do you think the problem could be solved?

That afternoon, Mrs Marigold did three jobs.

First she rang Sunnyside School and spoke to the principal.

Then she watered her garden with "Blush", the plant food for fantastically fast-blooming and fragrant flowers.

Lastly, she made herself a cup of tea and took Captain Rainbow on her knee. "I've been meaning to talk to you about your manners for a while now, Captain Rainbow," she said.

On Tuesday when the mayor arrived, a crowd of people gathered across the road to welcome him. They clapped and cheered as he got out of his car.

Everybody was happy. The bad leg on the centipede was at last going to be cleaned up.

But at number 27 . . .

Alliteration:

Repetition of initial sounds that creates a noticeable effect.

Which example of text includes alliteration?

A . . . she rang Sunnyside School and spoke to the principal

B . . . food for fantastically fast-blooming and fragrant flowers

A or B?

. . . Mrs Marigold's garden was in glorious bloom. The air was alive with perfumes and the singing of the birds.

In the long grass, children fed and played with rabbits and guinea pigs. The Royal Family spread its feathers in a brilliant display of colour.

The mayor, straight backed and stern, walked up the path.

"Hello, Mr Mayor. Lovely day. Hello, Mr Mayor. Lovely day," called Captain Rainbow from the porch.

Mrs Marigold sat on the porch in the middle of an excited group of children.

"What are the favourite foods of rabbits?"

"How long do parrots live?"

"How big do goldfish grow?"

Antonym:

An antonym is a word that means the opposite of another word.

Which word is the antonym for brilliant?

A   dull
B   beautiful
C   ordinary

A, B or C?

The mayor talked to Mrs Marigold, he talked to the children, and he talked to their teacher. He asked all sorts of questions. He looked into untrimmed hedges and unpruned trees. He walked through tangled grass and vines and tried to count the number of animals in the garden. He stayed for a whole hour.

Captain Rainbow perched on the letterbox as the mayor climbed into his car. "Goodbye, Sir! Drive carefully! Goodbye, Sir! Drive carefully!" he called.

Character Profile:

Which words would you use to describe the character of Mrs Marigold?

bossy
creative
mean
gentle
calm
prejudiced

The whole street waited for the mayor's decision. "Won't it be wonderful?" said the woman in Number 31. "No more untidy lawns, no more bedraggled hedges or ugly trees, no more nasty rabbits and guinea pigs, no more messy peacocks. Won't our street be perfect!"

On Thursday morning, a yellow council van pulled up at the gate.
A workman nailed a big white board to the lamp post. He put a letter into Mrs Marigold's box and then drove off.

"Look!" called the man in the house across the road. "Mrs Marigold's got her marching orders from the mayor."

"I'll bet it's a tidy-up-or-leave notice," said Mr Oglebump.

"I hope it's a demolition notice," grumbled Mr Symes. But it wasn't either of these. The sign said:

PROTECTED
All animals and plants
in this garden
are protected
by law.
The Mayor

Question:

Why do you think the mayor wanted to protect Mrs Marigold's garden?

That afternoon when the children came visiting, Mrs Marigold showed them the sign and read the letter she had received.

Dear Mrs Marigold,

Thank you for the wonderful afternoon I spent looking at your garden. Your garden is different but it is beautiful. I have decided to make it a children's reserve so that all the plants and animals are protected.

I will visit again soon. Your garden makes me stop thinking about all the hard work I've got to do. We can talk about how to stop your pets straying and upsetting your neighbours.

Your friend,
Archibald Snooks. (The Mayor)

When evening came, Mrs Marigold put her fingers to her mouth and sent out an ear-splitting whistle. It echoed into every nook and cranny in the neighbourhood. Home came the rabbits and guinea pigs. Home came the peacocks.

Home to celebrate.

Summary:

What key points would you put in a summary of *Mrs Marigold's Menagerie?*

- Mrs Marigold lives in a house with an untidy garden and a lot of animals.

- The neighbours complain to the mayor about Mrs Marigold.

- Mrs Marigold has an old terrier called Mop.

- Mrs Marigold invites children to come and visit the garden.

- The children feed and play with the animals in the garden.

- Mrs Marigold gets a letter from the mayor.

- The mayor comes to visit Mrs Marigold's house and decides that her garden is beautiful and that it – and the animals – should be protected.

Think about the Text

Making connections — talk about the connections you can make to the story *Mrs Marigold's Menagerie.*

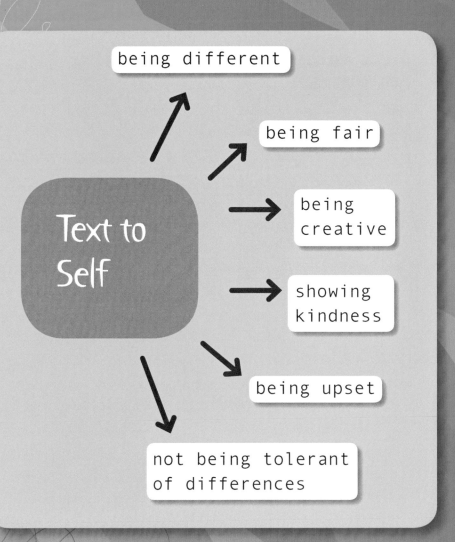

being different

being fair

Text to Self

being creative

showing kindness

being upset

not being tolerant of differences

Text to Text

Talk about other stories you may have read that have similar features. Compare the stories.

Text to World

Talk about situations in the world that might connect to elements in the story.

Planning a Short Story

1 ## Decide on a storyline

> Mrs Marigold has problems with her neighbours who do not like her untidy garden and her many animals.

> The neighbours complain about Mrs Marigold to the mayor, and he plans a visit to her house to check things out.

> Mrs Marigold invites all her friends to visit on the same day, and gives her garden plant food so it will be in full bloom.

> The major visits and talks to the children and Mrs Marigold. He is very impressed by the garden and animals.

> The mayor makes Mrs Marigold's garden a reserve to protect it by law.

2 ## Think about the characters

Think about the way they will think, act and feel. Make some short notes or quick sketches.

Mrs Marigold	Neighbours	The Mayor

creative
kind
eccentric

prejudiced
judgemental
unforgiving

fair
supportive
responsible

Decide on setting or settings
Make some short notes.

Decide on the events in order

Mrs Marigold's neighbours complain about her untidy garden and animals.

Introduction

Events

The neighbours write a letter of complaint to the mayor.

Conclusion

Short stories usually have . . .

A   A short introduction that grabs the reader's interest.

B   Fewer characters than longer stories.

C   A single fast-moving plot.

D   A climax that occurs late in the story.